LIFE IN EXTREME ENVIRONMENTS™

LIFE ON THE EQUATOR

STEPHANIE LAZOR

rosen
central™

The Rosen Publishing Group, Inc., New York

Published in 2004 by The Rosen Publishing Group, Inc.
29 East 21st Street, New York, NY 10010

Library of Congress Cataloging-in-Publication Data

Lazor, Stephanie.
Life on the equator/Stephanie Lazor.— 1st ed.
    p. cm.—(Life in extreme environments)
Summary: Defines the equator and indicates how plants, animals, and humans learn to survive in this extreme environment.
Includes bibliographical references and index.
ISBN 0-8239-3986-3 (lib. bdg.)
1. Natural history—Tropics. [1. Natural history—Tropics.
2. Ecology—Tropics. 3. Ecology.]
I. Title. II. Series.
QH84.5.L38 2004
910'.0213—dc21

                                        2003004029

Manufactured in the United States of America

CONTENTS

INTRODUCTION: JOURNEY TO THE CENTER OF THE EARTH

If you close your eyes and try to picture what the equator looks like, what do you see? Maybe a dotted line crossing through the earth like the ones depicted on world maps. By definition, the equator is a huge imaginary circle around the earth that is equal in distance from the two geographical poles—the North and South Poles. It forms the base line from which latitude is measured on maps (latitude is the angular distance north or south of the earth's equator, measured in degrees along a meridian, such as on a map or globe). If you were to run your finger along a map, you'd find the equator at zero degrees latitude, smack in the middle of the earth, intersecting South America, central Africa, and Indonesia.

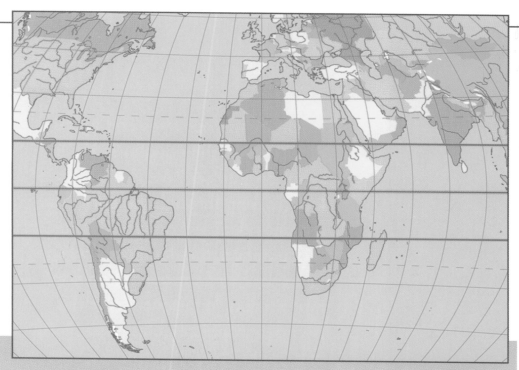

The parts of the earth that lie along the equator and between the tropics of Capricorn and Cancer (the blue lines north and south of the equator) are called the tropics. This area receives the most direct light and heat from the sun of anywhere on Earth. This means that there are no cool seasons like fall and winter, only periodic rainy seasons and dry seasons.

The equator, however, is much more than an imaginary line that is drawn on a map or globe. Imagine a place where the temperature never changes and a steady downpour of rain falls nearly twenty-four hours a day. Imagine, for example, it being summer twelve months a year with air as thick with heat and humidity at night as it is during the day. Now picture walking on a slippery carpet of wet, rotten leaves. You look up and instead of blue sky and white clouds all you can see is a tight canopy of green leaves. Only a thin slice of sky peeks through the thick mass of tree branches. Growing on the trees are brightly colored exotic flowers. You hear the constant sound of insects and birds in the background. You might even see an occasional gorilla or jaguar lurking around. This is an equatorial rain forest.

This tropical environment has such an extraordinary number of plants and animals that it is possible you would see hundreds of different species in a matter of minutes. The incredible number of living things here is one of the major differences between equatorial rain forests and the forests of North America.

Now picture yourself in a region where the changes in altitude are as extreme as the contrasts in climate. Imagine being in an environment that contains almost every known landform on earth—from glacial ice to dry deserts, mountain massifs to tropical grasslands, immense lakes to forests thick with trees. Almost daily you find yourself surrounded by herds of elephant wading in the shallow rivers, or crocodiles basking in the heat of the sun while other amazing animals such as gazelles, giraffes, and zebras wander around you on the banks. If this is where you find yourself, you are probably in one of the nature reserves found on a savannah in Kenya, a country that lies on the equator.

These unpredictable and unusual conditions are just part of the reason why life near the equator can be considered life in an extreme environment.

CHAPTER ONE

WHAT IS THE EQUATOR?

Simply put, the equator is an imaginary line that divides the earth into two halves, known as the Northern and Southern Hemispheres. Its purpose is to help locate places and determine direction on a map.

THE TROPICS

The other two significant lines on a map are the tropic of Cancer and the tropic of Capricorn. Of the three lines, the equator is the longest line of latitude on the earth. It crosses through Colombia, Brazil, São Tomé and Principe, Gabon,

This black rhinoceros mingles with cape buffalo on the Masai Mara in Kenya. Rhinoceros means "horn nosed." For millions of years, black rhinos have used their horns for protection against lions and other predators and as weapons in territorial disputes with other rhinos.

Republic of the Congo, Democratic Republic of the Congo, Uganda, Kenya, Somalia, the Maldives, Indonesia, Kiribati, and the appropriately named Ecuador. The tropics each lie at 23.5° latitude. The tropic of Cancer is located at 23.5° latitude north of the equator and runs through Mexico, the Bahamas, Egypt, Saudi Arabia, India, and southern China, as well as many other countries. The tropic of Capricorn lies at 23.5° south of the equator, and it runs through Australia, Chile, southern Brazil, and northern South Africa. Brazil is the only country in the world that is intersected by both the equator and a tropic.

THE FOUR SEASONS

The sun is directly above the tropics twice during a calendar year, which determines the beginning of winter and summer. On June 21, when the sun is directly overhead at noon at the tropic of Cancer, it is officially summer in the Northern Hemisphere and winter in the Southern Hemisphere. When the sun is directly above the tropic of Cancer on December 21, it is the beginning of winter in the

DID YOU KNOW?

The equator is 24,902 miles (40,075 kilometers) long, crosses over the span of three oceans, and passes through thirteen countries.

Northern Hemisphere and the beginning of summer in the Southern Hemisphere.

The area between the tropics of Capricorn and Cancer that surrounds the equator is known as the tropics. This region does not experience a change in seasons because the sun is constantly overhead. Only higher latitudes located north and south of the tropics experience significant seasonal differences in climate. At the equator, the climate is warm and abnormally humid with plenty of sunshine and more rainfall than any other area of the world. The majority of the earth's tropical rain forests—forests of tall trees in a region where there is at least 100 inches (254 centimeters) of rain per year, and it is warm all year round—exist near the equator. However, to the surprise of some, the equator is more than just a tropical environment with blazing temperatures.

TROPICAL GRASSLANDS

There are also dry areas along the equator. Savannahs, which are tropical grasslands, are also found there. While savannahs are located at tropical latitudes, they are much drier than rain forests.

Rainfall levels in the savannahs are between 20 and 60 inches (51 to 152 cm) a year, and the rainy season usually occurs during the same time each year. This is very different

This is the Orinoco Savannah in Colombia. The Orinoco basin of Venezuela and Colombia includes grass savannahs (called *llanos*) maintained by the annual flooding of the Orinoco River and long periods of standing water that prevent trees from growing.

from the precipitation in a rain forest, where there is a total of 80 to 160 inches (203 to 406 cm) of rain each year. Weather conditions in this region reach both extremes—after the immense rainfall, long periods of drought follow.

Unlike the rain forests, which are populated primarily with trees, the dominant forms of plant life in savannahs are grasses and small plants. Trees are sparse throughout this semi-arid landscape, growing only where there are cracks in the surface or deep soil.

VOLCANOES

Another example of how the equator is a complex environment filled with extremes is the Masai Mara National Reserve at the southwest corner of Kenya. This region defies the usual image of the equatorial tropics. Instead of tropical rain forests, Masai Mara is filled with woodlands and savannahs. How is this possible in the tropics?

Two million years ago, volcanic activity pushed up the lush forest floors of this region, creating a plateau 5,000 feet (1,524 meters) above sea level. At this elevation, the warm ocean winds were cut off, the forests disappeared, and ash from the volcano settled over the highlands, creating the rolling plains that occupy this area today. At this region of the equator, temperatures can rise to as much as 100° Fahrenheit (38° Celsius) and can drop to as low as 50°F (10° C).

This kind of dramatic volcanic activity also created Mount Kenya. Once taller than Mount Everest, which stands at 29,035 feet (8,850 m), Mount Kenya has shrunk to just 17,000 feet (5,181 m) in the last century and is now crowned with snow.

The equator is such an extreme environment that even though it is hot and humid 365 days a year, snow can exist as well. You may be wondering why snow doesn't melt at the

equator. That's because the temperature decreases as you get higher than sea level. In fact, for every 1,000 feet (305 m), the temperature drops approximately 5.5°F (3°C). Also, the shiny surface of the snow reflects the sun's rays, keeping the snow frozen. This is called the albedo effect. And, because the snow is so deeply packed at the peak of the mountain, the lower layers of snow cool the surface layer, which counteracts the warming effects of the sun.

Mount Kenya, which is on the equator, experiences many rainy periods. The most rainfall occurs between late March and the middle of May, with slightly less than that between late October and mid-December. The most rainfall occurs in the forest belt and on the southeast side of the mountain, where rainfall levels can be up to 8 feet (2.5 m) per year. Rain and, at higher altitudes, snow, can occur at any time of the year. Temperatures vary considerably with height and with time of day. On the plains surrounding Mount Kenya, the average day temperature is about 77°F (25°C). Nighttime temperatures on the summit are well below freezing.

CHAPTER TWO

PLANT LIFE

A large majority of the equator's plant life can be found in the equatorial rain forests. Tropical rain forests are found in three major geographical areas, all of which are intersected by the equator: the Amazon River basin in South America, Africa, and Indo-Malaysia. Rain forests are characterized by forests of tall, dense trees in regions of warmth and plentiful rainfall.

You may wonder why such a hot environment, one that receives constant, direct rays from the sun 365 days a year, isn't a dry, sandy desert. This is because constant winds come in toward the equator from the North and South Poles.

A palmito tree in the Brazilian rain forest. They are harvested in the wild and grown on plantations for their soft inner cores, which are sold as heart of palm. Heart of palm is used in many recipes and as a nutritional supplement. Like many tropical plants, palmitos thrive in stable light, humidity, and temperature, and require regular rainfall.

These winds are filled with moisture. When they mix with the intense heat of the equator, they cause moisture to rise, cool, and then create rain. It can rain almost twenty-four hours a day in most tropical areas. In some regions, there can be more than 15 feet (5 m) of rain a year. By comparison, Los Angeles, California, receives only about 7 inches of rain (177 millimeters) per year.

There is at least one "dry" month a year in this environment, but if you visited a tropical rain forest during this period, you would see it is still astonishingly wet. Because this environment has such an extraordinary amount of rainfall, even the slightest break in rain is considered a dry period.

While rain forests cover less than 7 percent of the earth's surface, they are home to more types of trees than any other area in the world. In fact, scientists have counted about 280 different species of trees in a 2.5-acre area of South America alone.

LAYERS OF THE RAIN FOREST

Trees are the main form of plant life in the rain forest. A tropical rain forest consists of four layers: the emergent trees, the canopy, the understory, and the forest floor. The emergent and canopy layers make up the top of the rain forest, where trees poke out above the green growth to reach the sun. Since the majority of plant growth occurs in the sun, most rain forest animals live in the canopy layer, which gives them easy access to food and the shade of the plants.

Below the top layers are the young trees and shrubs that make up the understory. The plants here rarely grow to large sizes because the canopy layer blocks most of the sunlight. The forest floor is practically bare because only a small amount of sunlight can get through to the ground. Large mammals, such as Asian elephants, that are too heavy to climb up into the upper layers live on the forest floor.

Three female Asian elephants and a calf cool off in the Rajaji National Park in India. Asian elephants live in forests in India, Nepal, Bhutan, Bangladesh, Sri Lanka, Burma, Thailand, Cambodia, Laos, Vietnam, Malaysia, Indonesia, and Borneo. They can be found in many types of tropical climates—savannahs, rain forests, or deciduous forests.

SAVANNAHS

When many people imagine a savannah, they think of a dry environment. However, savannahs are more than just heat and dry air. It is the combination of forest weather and desert climate that makes this environment different. Savannahs are areas in dry tropics and subtropics in which many types of tall grasses (such as elephant grass), along with scattered leafy trees, are the main form of plant life. Savannahs are usually found on either side of rain forests. There is extensive savannah covering tropical and subtropical areas of central and southern Africa, central South America, India, and parts of Australia. There are only three seasons in this region: cool and dry, hot and dry, and warm and wet.

Trees and Grasses of the Savannah

Much like rain forests, savannahs are home to many different and interesting plants and animals. Plant life in the savannah is

able to grow under hot, seasonally dry climatic conditions and is characterized by scattered trees, which are usually thorny and small-leaved. Many of these trees are kinds of acacias. The most popular tree in this region, however, is the gigantic baobab, which has the second largest trunk diameter of all other tree species except for the sequoia. The life span of this massive tree is more than one thousand years.

The African baobab tree is one of the largest trees in the world. It can grow to a height of 82 feet (25 m), with a diameter of 39 feet (12 m). This massive tree, also called the "dead rat tree" because of the rodent-like long and hairy fruits that dangle from its branches, can live for over 1,000 years.

Epiphyte orchids, like this *Cattleya aclandiae* from Brazil, grow on top of other plants, usually trees. In Greek, *epi* means "on top of," and *phyte* means "plant." Epiphytes will not grow in soil, and they need air around their roots to survive.

Although savannahs have trees and a few bushes, the most dominant plants are grasses. In fact, 50 percent of the plants in the savannah are grasses. These grasses are kept low by grazers like the wildebeest and, in some places, water buffalo. Because there are frequent fires in the savannah, the dominant vegetation is fire adapted, but many seedlings are killed—either by fire or grazing animals—before they become established.

The plant life in equatorial savannahs has had to adapt in order to survive. Bushes and trees have developed small leathery leaves that can resist drought and intense heat. Because there is a great deal of sunshine, the plants must also have sufficient moisture to survive.

RAIN FOREST EPIPHYTES

Epiphytes—plants such as orchids, ferns, mosses, and lichens that grow piggyback on top of taller trees—are interesting plants that go to extreme lengths to survive in rain forests. Epiphytes grow on top of the trees in the upper layers of the forest so they can receive the plentiful sunlight and rainfall that is not found in the lower layers. For this reason, epiphytes are commonly called air plants.

Rain forest plants need to adjust to such an extreme environment. The special characteristics that enable plants and animals to be successful in a particular environment are called adaptations. With more than ninety days and at least 100 inches (254 cm) of rain per year in a rain forest, rot, growth of mold, and decay can occur. Like plants on the savannah, plants in the rain forest have developed adaptations, such as slick, water-repellent coatings on leaves and spoutlike "drip tips" that enable them to shed water efficiently. Also, because the rain forest has poor soil with few nutrients, native plants typically do not produce flowers, which helps them preserve energy.

BENEFITS OF RAIN FOREST PLANTS

About one-fourth of all the medicines we use in the world today come from equatorial rain forests. These plants can do a lot more than help with the common cold or be used to make ointments for scrapes and cuts. The National Cancer Institute has identified three thousand species of plants in the entire world that have anticancer properties. Of these three thousand species, 70 percent are from rain forests. More

than two thousand varieties of tropical plants are thought to be possible cures for cancer. The rosy periwinkle, for example, is used in the treatment of certain types of leukemia. Additionally, quinine, which comes from a rain forest tree called cinchona, is used to treat malaria. Curare, an extract from a tropical vine found in the South American rain forest, is used as an anesthetic and to relax muscles during surgery.

Chicle, the original base for chewing gum, comes from the chicle tree, which grows from southern Mexico to northern Brazil. The sap is molded into blocks and processed by adding sugar and flavoring. Today, chicle has been largely replaced with the sap from other trees and by synthetic gums.

Approximately $10 billion worth of rain forest products—including rattan, nuts and spices, and bamboo—are purchased each year. Believe it or not, bamboo is the largest type of grass. It is very fast growing, reaching its full height in only two to three months. Bamboo physically adapts to its environment by growing tall quickly so that it is able to receive a lot of sunlight and rain.

Bengal bamboo is important to its tropical environment because it can reduce soil erosion by sucking up water from heavy tropical rains. It is one of the most useful species of bamboo and can grow anywhere between 40 and 60 feet (12 to 18 m) in height and is approximately 3 inches (eight cm) wide at maturity.

Although rain forests may seem like faraway places, many of the plants in your own home come from there. Common houseplants, such as bromeliads, African violets, and the Christmas cactus, originate there. Also, foods such as bananas, avocados, pineapples, and chocolate come from equatorial rain forests.

In the United States, the average forest contains from five to twelve different kinds of trees. In a typical rain forest, on the other hand, there may be more than three hundred different species. Rain forests usually contain ten times more types of trees and five times more bird species than temperate forests. In fact, the Amazon rain forest in South America is home to more than 1,600 species of birds and about a million different kinds of insects.

CHAPTER THREE

ANIMAL KINGDOM

Areas near the equator, such as rain forests and savannahs, are home to many of the strangest looking animals on Earth. They are also home to the most beautiful, the largest, the smallest, the most frightening, the least dangerous, the loudest, and the quickest animals.

ANIMALS OF THE RAIN FOREST

There are many different species of animals that live near the equator. They include jaguars, toucans, gorillas, parrots, and even tarantulas, as well

A lioness patiently endures her cub's playful behavior on the Masai Mara National Reserve in Kenya. There are about twenty resident lion prides in the Masai Mara, the highest density being in the Musiara Marsh area. Lions are the dominant predator on the African savannah.

The okapi is the only known living relative of the giraffe. "Okapi" is a corruption of the native name *o'api*. Standing about 5 to 5 1/2 feet (150 to 170 cm) tall at the shoulder, the okapi is a dark chestnut brown or purplish red in color, with horizontal stripes on its upper legs. It eats leaves, grasses, and fruit, and it can be found in the Ituri Forest in the northeastern region of the Democratic Republic of the Congo. Its main predator is the leopard.

as more exotic animals such as the aye-aye and the okapi. There are so many species of animals in rain forests that millions have yet to be identified.

Why do more species of animals live in rain forests than other parts of the world? For example, 90 percent of all primates are found in tropical forests. Scientists believe this is because the rain forests are the oldest ecosystem on Earth. Some forests in Southeast Asia have existed for at least 100 million years, ever since dinosaurs roamed the earth. When the Ice Age occurred, the frozen areas of the North and South Poles covered much of the earth, causing huge numbers of extinctions. But this giant freeze did not reach many of the rain forests, and while there aren't any dinosaurs left, millions of other animals that thrived there continue to evolve.

Another reason for the extraordinary number of species in this region is the nearly perfect living conditions. Because there is a constant temperature of 75°F to 80°F (24°C to 27°C), animals will not freeze during cold winters or burn from lack of shade in the hot summers. With rainfall occurring almost every day, they also don't have to search for water.

ANIMALS OF THE SAVANNAH

A great variety of animal life can be found living in savannahs. The savannah is full of mammals like tigers, gazelles, and zebras and also has amphibians such as the African tree frog. Additionally, hundreds of birds call the savannah their home. Among the most

THE WHITE RHINO

If one of the white rhino's nose horns is broken off, it will grow back! The horns can grow from 1 to 3 inches (2.5 to 8 cm) in a year. The longest rhino horn known was more than 5 feet (1.5 m) long!

Stick and leaf insects, as their name implies, are a type of insect whose bodies resemble sticks or leaves. There are around 2,700 known species, which mainly come from the tropics, though there are 3 New Zealand species and about 20 European species. The longest insect in the world is a stick insect called *Pharnacia kirbyi*, which can grow to a length of 22 inches (555 mm)!

common birds found here are the flamingo, marabou stork, and the vulture. Other animals that dominate the savannah are elephants, black rhinoceros, and cheetahs.

King of the Savannah

Perhaps, the most famous predatory animal living in savannahs is the lion. These golden-colored felines can grow to be as much as 6 feet (1.8 m) long and weigh up to 420 pounds (190 kilograms). The average life span of the lion is approximately fifteen years in the wild. Lions live in permanent groups, called prides, which can have up to twenty-five lions in them. Female lions do most of the hunting, often in groups.

INSECTS

Insects are the largest single animal group living in tropical rain forests. If you visited a rain forest, it wouldn't be very likely that you would run into too many monkeys

Though it may seem hard to believe, even penguins can be found on the equator. The Galápagos penguin inhabits the equatorial shores of the Isabela and Fernandina Islands off the coast of Ecuador. The Galápagos is the third smallest of the world's penguin species.

or jaguars. But you would be sure to see millions of insects crawling around in all four layers of the rain forest. They include brightly colored butterflies, pesky mosquitoes, camouflaged stick insects, and huge colonies of ants. Scientists estimate that more than fifty million different types of invertebrates live in rain forests. One scientist found fifty different species of ants on a single tree in Peru.

Many invertebrates live in the savannah as well. Grasshoppers, which can hop, walk, and fly, are one example.

There are about ten thousand different species of grasshoppers. Other insects in the savannah include ants, beetles, and termites.

FIGHT FOR SURVIVAL

The search for food, sunlight, and space is a constant struggle in rain forests. However, it is actually this fierce competition that enables so many animals to live together. It is also the reason there are so many different species living in these regions. The secret is in the ability of many animals to adapt to eating a specific plant or animal that few other species are able to eat.

For example, parrots and toucans have enormous beaks that give them an advantage over birds with much smaller ones. The fruits and nuts from many trees in this area have evolved with tough shells, which protect them from predators. The unusually large beaks that parrots and toucans have developed act as nutcrackers, providing them with meals other birds can't access.

Each species of animal in the rain forest has unique adaptations to help it survive and protect itself from becoming something else's next meal. An example of this is the ability to camouflage. The coloring of some animals acts as protection

The toco is the largest of the toucan family, with a large lightweight beak and a body about 25 inches (63.5 cm) long. The bright colors on its beak and body may be used to attract mates. The toucan also has a narrow tongue used for eating small fruits and insects off trees. Because of its large beak, the toucan is a poor flier and spends most of its time in hollow trees.

from their predators. One example is the walking stick, a type of insect that looks like a twig. It blends in so well with the trees that you wouldn't notice it unless it moved. And some butterflies, when they close their wings, look just like leaves.

Camouflage also works in reverse, helping predators sneak up on their prey. However, rain forest animals must not only hide from their predators in order to survive but must also be noticed by the mates they depend on for reproduction, which can be a challenge.

ADAPTATIONS OF SAVANNAH ANIMALS

Animals living in savannahs also need to adapt in order to survive in their extreme environment. Because a constant food supply is not a given in the savannah, animals that live there have adapted to a great deal of variability in the food supply throughout the year. At times there is plenty of food (during and after the wet season), while at other times there is almost no food or water (during the dry season). Because of this, many savannah animals survive by migrating.

THE CHEETAH

While most big cats are able to chase their prey only a few hundred meters, the cheetah chases for 3.4 miles (5,500 m) at an average speed of 45 miles per hour (72 km per hour).

A specific example of a savannah animal that has had to adapt to its environment is the cheetah. This fierce animal has adapted by having the ability to pursue its prey at high speeds. This is important because the cheetah relies on sight rather than smell to spot its prey, and it can target animals from far distances.

ENDANGERED SPECIES

Despite their adaptations, animals that live near the equator are in grave danger of becoming extinct. In fact, an average of thirty-five animal species become extinct in equatorial rain forests every day. The dangers equatorial animals (particularly those found in rain forests and savannahs) face include logging, cattle ranching, and human overpopulation. In rain forests in particular, the loss of millions of acres of land forces animals and humans out of their homes when trees are cut down. And sadly, most animals die when the forest is destroyed.

Extinction in Rain Forests

When rain forests are destroyed, the effects are wide reaching. Animals that live outside the tropics suffer as well. Songbirds, hummingbirds, warblers, and thousands of other North American birds spend their winters in rain forests, returning to the same location year after year. Fewer return to the north

A jaguar stalks its prey in Belize, home to the world's only jaguar preserve. The third largest member of the cat family, the jaguar is endangered in most of its habitats. Jaguars eat turtles, young crocodiles, and fish, as well as birds and monkeys. They were once worshiped as gods by South and Central American cultures such as the Aztecs, the Olmecs, and the Maya. The name "jaguar" comes from a native word meaning "the killer that takes its prey in a single bound."

each spring because fewer survive through the winter once their habitat has been destroyed.

The cutting down of trees is not the only reason animals are becoming extinct in rain forests. Thousands of monkeys and other primates—wanted for their fur, as pets, or for scientific research—are traded illegally each year. Parrots and macaws have also become popular pets. Even the jaguar, the king of the jungle, is in danger of becoming extinct because its fur is highly valuable for making coats and shoes.

The rate of extinction among rain forest animals is as astonishing as the extraordinary number of species that can be found in this small region of the world. The rate at which rain forest animals are becoming extinct in equatorial rain forests has never been as high as it is now.

Extinction in Savannahs

Many savannahs have been destroyed by humans who are looking for new environments in which to live. In fact, in the last two hundred years, many animals that once lived on savannahs have lost their habitats and become extinct. An example of an animal in danger of extinction is the white rhinoceros, whose name means "nose horn." This savannah mammal is a large, thick skinned, gray rhinoceros with two nose horns. It can be found roaming in the grassy plains of Africa near the equator. A person might think that rhinos are safe from extinction because the only other mammal that can kill an adult rhino is a human. Nonetheless, rhinos, and in particular the white rhino, are in grave danger because of poachers who sell their horns to use in medicines.

CHAPTER FOUR

WALKING THE LINE

Centuries ago, explorers believed that life at the equator was impossible because of the intense heat from the sun. They figured that the sun's rays would be so strong that anyone who went near the equator would be burned to ashes almost immediately. They also believed that the seas would boil and that the air would catch fire. It wasn't until 1473, when Portuguese explorers managed to sail all the way to the equator and back without being burned alive, that people began to realize that it was possible to live at the equator.

Most of the equator crosses oceans, especially the Pacific Ocean, but parts of northern South America, central Africa, and Southeast Asia are directly on the equator. In fact, there are 534 million people who live at or near the equator.

Indigenous, or native, people have called rain forests and savannahs their homes for thousands of years. There are approximately 250 million indigenous people in the world today, belonging to more than five thousand groups and living in more than seventy countries worldwide. The rain forests alone are home to an estimated 50 million indigenous people.

While many people on the equator live much like we do in North America, some still live as their ancestors did many years before them. These groups organize their daily lives differently than other cultures because of the environment in which they live. Everything they need to survive, from food to medicine to clothing, comes from their environment.

FOOD

People who live in the equatorial rain forests survive by hunting, gathering fruits and nuts, and fishing. They also, however, plant small gardens for other sources of food, using a farming method in which they clear a small area of land and burn it. This type of farming is called slash-and-burn agriculture. They grow many types of plants that will be used for food and medicine. However, this method of farming can have a devastating effect on rain forests.

A Yanomami hunter draws his bow. The Yanomami are an indigenous tribe (also called Yanamamo, Yanomam, and Sanuma) made up of four subdivisions of tribespeople who live in the tropical rain forests of southern Venezuela and northern Brazil.

THE MASAI

The equatorial lands of Kenya are home to Kenya's most famous tribe, the Masai. They are known for their fearsome reputation as warrior and their harmonious relationship with their environment. They are forbidden to eat wild animals and they do not farm the land around them. Instead, they share it with the wild animals, who are already there. The Masai culture is based on their cattle—their wealth is based on the size of their herds. They are nomads who wander from region to region looking for places where their herds can graze. Their diet consists of fresh and curdled milk, carried and stored in long decorated gourds. They add blood from their cattle to the milk. For meat, they will slaughter a sheep or a goat, but they kill cows only for ceremonies.

The houses of the Masai are mostly constructed from cattle manure, or dung. They build small rectangular huts that are arranged in a circle and surrounded by a thorn fence to protect livestock from predators, such as lions. Many of the older men in the tribes have more than one wife, and men of the same age group typically share their wives. Jewelry, dress, and hairstyle (for both men and women) are extremely important to the Masai, as it indicates their status.

EDUCATION

Most children who live in tribes do not attend conventional schools. Instead, their parents and other tribe members educate them about the environment in which they live. They are taught how to survive by learning how to hunt and fish and by

Masai women are in charge of building their huts. The huts are made of branches, twigs, cow dung, and urine that is formed into a plaster and applied to a branch frame. When dry, the mixture is strong as cement and doesn't smell. They also spend much time doing bead work. They decorate animal hides, gourds, and make beaded jewelry including arm and leg bracelets and amulets.

learning which plants are useful as medicine or food. Some of these children know more about rain forests or savannahs than scientists who have studied those regions for many years.

In the Masai tribe, men as young as fourteen are considered "morans," or warriors. They move up in status on an average of every fifteen years, from junior warriors, senior warriors, and junior elders, until they eventually become the decision makers of the tribe, known as senior elders. Between the ages of fourteen and around thirty, the morans herd the cattle throughout the savannah and live separately from the rest of the tribe. It is not until they are junior elders that they are allowed to have a wife. At this time, the men are between thirty and thirty-five, and the women are fourteen or fifteen.

The Kenyan government is trying to encourage the Masai to find permanent homes and to discontinue the practice of having morans live separately so that they can have formal education.

DANGER FOR RAIN FOREST INHABITANTS

The dangers indigenous people living in rain forests face are as complex as the environment they inhabit. Rain forest inhabitants have been losing the land they live on, and their lives, for more than five hundred years—ever since Europeans began colonizing. The majority of these early settlers died from common European diseases, like the flu, which made them very sick or killed them because they had never been exposed to these diseases before. Also, foreigners who invaded the rain forests went to severe measures to secure the land they were after, and in the process they killed many of the people who lived there. The indigenous people were even put to work as slaves to harvest the resources of the forest. Others were forced to give up their cultural traditions by Christian missionaries who made them convert to Christianity.

Indigenous groups are becoming more intent on fighting for their land. Most often, they do this through peaceful demonstrations that have severe consequences, such as being arrested or even the loss of their lives. For example, the Kayapo Indians of Brazil recently spoke before the United States Congress to protest the building of dams in the Amazon rain forest and were arrested when they arrived back in Brazil. Those who are in the equatorial rain forests will continue to protest because they know that taking no action could lead to the most devastating ramification of all—the loss of their land and culture forever.

CHAPTER FIVE

FRAGILE: HANDLE WITH CARE

The equatorial regions described in the previous chapters of the book are in extreme trouble. Savannahs, for example, are in danger of becoming wiped out by desertification—the process by which areas of desert are created by the destruction of natural forests or by the activities of developers. If this continues, these tropical grasslands could all turn into deserts. Perhaps the equatorial region that is in most danger, however, is the rain forests.

DEFORESTATION

The process in which a forest is cut down, burned, or otherwise damaged is called deforestation. Scientists say that anywhere from 13 million to 55 million acres of tropical rain forests are destroyed every year. Many people do not know the harm that occurs when tropical rain forests are destroyed. One of the major harms is the excess amount of carbon dioxide that remains in the air. Trees and plants use carbon dioxide to make food—part of a process called photosynthesis. However, too much carbon dioxide in the air can be a big problem.

Carbon dioxide is a heavy gas that holds heat and causes the temperature of the surrounding area to rise. Because the trees and plants that use carbon dioxide are being destroyed, the levels of the gas in the atmosphere are increasing.

THE GREENHOUSE EFFECT

The destruction of tropical rain forests is steadily contributing to the greenhouse effect. The greenhouse effect raises the temperature all around the world. This is known as global warming. Scientists say that if this continues, there will be a rise in temperature, ice at the poles will melt, and sea levels will rise, affecting millions of people with major flooding. We are also in

Rain forest is burned in Brazil to clear land for cattle ranching. Many poor people use slash-and-burn methods to clear land for farming or ranching. Besides hurting the environment, this method is also very ineffective because of the poor soils in rain forests, which will not yield much in the way of crops or feed.

danger of losing some of the most beautiful areas in the world. If the current rate of deforestation continues, rain forests will be gone within one hundred years. This could cause unknown effects to the world's climate, not to mention the elimination of the majority of plant and animal life on the planet.

HOW DEFORESTATION HAPPENS

Deforestation occurs in many ways. The majority of the rain forest that is cut down is used for agricultural use—as grazing land for cattle and for planting crops. Poor farmers cut down a small area, usually a few acres, and burn the tree trunks. This is what was referred to earlier as slash-and-burn agriculture.

In modern agriculture, much larger areas of rain forests are cleared away at a time, sometimes deforesting several square miles at once. Rain forests are often replaced as large cattle pastures in order to raise cattle, which in turn can provide beef for the world's population.

WHY DEFORESTATION HAPPENS

Why would anyone deliberately cut down the rain forests when it can cause such enormous damage to the earth? There are many different reasons. For example, a great number of tropical countries are extremely poor and have a great need

Brazilian mahogany is a prized hardwood among furniture makers because of its durability and beautiful color. The Brazilian government is supposed to regulate mahogany harvesting to ensure it does not harm the environment, but many environmental groups believe that illegal harvesting continues.

for money. The government sells logging concessions to raise money for projects, to pay debts, or to develop industry. Brazil, for example, had a national debt of $195 billion in 1995 for which payments had to be made each year. Brazil can make a profit by selling the right to cut down valuable hardwoods, such as mahogany, to logging companies.

Also, peasant farmers often cut down rain forests to raise crops so that they can feed themselves and their families. Most tropical countries are poor compared to the United States and Canada, and farming is a basic way of life for a large part of the population. Farmers in these poor countries do not have the money to buy necessities, so they have to raise crops for food and to sell. However, because the rain forest soil is so poor in nutrients, the farmers cannot reuse the land year after year. When the ground can no longer support crops, the farmers move on to other sections of the forest and clear away more land, destroying the rain forest in the process. The land abandoned by farmers is left to grow back to a rain forest. However, the forest will grow slowly because of the lack of nutrients in the soil. After the land is abandoned, the forest usually takes about fifty years to grow back.

EFFECTS OF DEFORESTATION

As was mentioned earlier, the equatorial rain forests are home to more than half of the world's plants and animals. Most of these species can only be found in small areas because they require a special habitat to live. Deforestation is especially dangerous to these plants and animals because if their habitat is destroyed, they may become extinct. Every

EXTINCTION

Scientists do not know the exact rate at which rain forest species are becoming extinct, but they estimate that thirty-five species disappear worldwide each day.

day, when the forests are being cut down, it means that many species are disappearing forever.

The loss of these species will have a great impact on the entire planet. We are losing organisms that could help us find cures for diseases such as cancer or AIDS. Because of human intervention, the earth loses millions of acres of rain forest each year. An area of rain forest the size of the states of New Hampshire and Vermont, for example, is cut down annually. As a result, less than 3.4 million square miles (5.4 million km) of forest remain today. Species that depend on rain forests cannot be replaced. Once the web of interdependence has been broken, plants and animals have no way to rebuild their complex communities.

FACTS ABOUT DEFORESTATION

- At the current rate of destruction, all the rain forests will be gone in less than one hundred years.

- More than 50 percent of the original rain forests have been cut down.

- Thirty-five species become extinct per day due to rain forest damage.

- Every second, 2.4 acres of rain forest are cut down (this is equal to two football fields).

For many reasons, what was once a lush, tropical environment filled with rare plant and animal life—not to mention the home of many indigenous tribes—has become farmland like that seen here.

- For each pound of beef produced for fast food, 220 square feet (20.4 sq m) of rain forest are burned.

- Tropical rain forests once covered more than 14 percent of the earth's land area but now cover less than 6 percent.

The environment surrounding the equator is among the most fascinating and complex in the world. With a climate of yearlong sun and heat and some of the most exotic animal species in existence, life on the equator requires many adaptations and survival techniques. It is true that the equator is, by definition, only an imaginary line intended to give direction and locate places. The environment, however, is responsible for much, much more—from saving lives with medical breakthroughs and advances, to supplying the entire world with clean, fresh air. So if you think the equator is a far and distant place that does not have an impact on your life, you are mistaken.

GLOSSARY

altitude The height of something above a reference level, especially above sea level or above the earth's surface.

arctic A region between the North Pole and the northern timberlines of North America and Eurasia.

arid Lacking moisture, especially having insufficient rainfall to support trees or woody plants.

canopy layer Second tallest layer of the rain forest that forms a tight canopy 60 to 90 feet (18 to 27 m) above the ground.

deforestation The cutting down and clearing away of trees or forests.

ecosystem An ecological community together with its environment, functioning as a unit.

emergent layer Top layer of the rain forest made up of giant trees that tower above the rest of the layers.

epiphyte A plant, such as a tropical orchid or a staghorn fern, that grows on another plant upon which it depends for mechanical support but not for nutrients.

erosion The group of natural processes, including weathering, dissolution, abrasion, corrosion, and transportation, by which material is worn away from the earth's surface.

extinct No longer existing or living.

Ice Age The most recent glacial period, which occurred during the Pleistocene glacial epoch.

indigenous Originating and living or occurring naturally in an area or environment.

invertebrate An animal that has no spinal column.

latitude The angular distance north or south of the earth's equator, measured in degrees along a meridian, as on a map or globe.

massif A large mountain mass or compact group of connected mountains, forming an independent portion of a range.

meridian An imaginary great circle on the earth's surface passing through the North and South Poles. All points on the same meridian have the same longitude.

Northern Hemisphere The half of the earth north of the equator.

North Pole The northern end of the the earth's axis of rotation; a point in the Arctic Ocean.

polar Relating to, connected with, or located near the North Pole or South Pole.

primate The highest order of mammals; includes man, together with the apes and monkeys.

rattan The stems of any of various climbing palms of the genera *Calamus, Daemonorops,* or *Plectomia* of tropical Asia, having long, tough, slender stems. It is used to make wickerwork, canes, and furniture.

reserve A reservation of public land set aside for the sake of preservation.

savannah   A flat grassland of tropical or subtropical regions.

Southern Hemisphere   The half of the earth south of the equator.

South Pole   The southern end of the earth's axis of rotation; a point in Antarctica.

species   A class of individuals or objects grouped by virtue of their common attributes and assigned a common name; a division subordinate to a genus.

tropical rain forest   A tropical forest with heavy annual rainfall.

tropic of Cancer   The parallel of latitude 23.5° north of the equator and the most northerly latitude at which the sun can shine directly overhead.

tropic of Capricorn   The parallel of latitude 23.5° south of the equator and the most southerly latitude at which the sun can shine directly overhead.

tropics   The region of the earth's surface lying between the tropics of Cancer and Capricorn.

understory   Third layer of the rain forest that contains young trees that have not yet grown tall enough to reach the emergent or canopy layers and also leafy plants that can survive in low light.

FOR MORE INFORMATION

Amazon Center for Environmental Education and Research
   (ACEER) Foundation
2070 Valleydale Road, Suite 1
Birmingham, AL 35244
(205) 985-0611
Web site: http://www.aceer.org

Rainforest Action Network
221 Pine Street, Suite 500
San Francisco, CA 94104
(415) 398-4404
Web site: http://www.ran.org

WEB SITES

Due to the changing nature of Internet links, the Rosen
Publishing Group, Inc., has developed an online list of Web
sites related to the subject of this book. This site is updated
regularly. Please use this link to access the list:

http://www.rosenlinks.com/lee/equa

FOR FURTHER READING

Berger, Melvin. *Does It Always Rain in the Rain Forest? Questions and Answers About Tropical Rain Forests.* New York: Scholastic, Inc., 2002.

George, Jean Craighead. *One Day in the Tropical Rain Forest.* New York: HarperCollins, 1995.

Twain, Mark. *Following the Equator: A Journey Around the World.* New York: Dover Publications, 1989.

BIBLIOGRAPHY

Allaby, Michael. *Biomes of the World, Volume 7*. Oxford, UK: Andromeda Limited, 1999.

Brown, Katrina. *The Causes of Tropical Deforestation*. London: UCL Press, 1994.

Kellert, Stephen R. Macmillon. *Encyclopedia of the Environment*. New York: Simon and Schuster and Prentice International, 1997.

Park, Chris. *Tropical Rainforests*. London: Routledge, 1992.

Richards, Paul. *The Tropical Rain Forest*. Cambridge, UK: Press Syndicate of the University of Cambridge, 1996.

"Savanna Animal Printouts." Enchanted Learning Online. Retrieved March 27, 2003 (http://www.enchantedlearning.com/biomes/savanna/savanna.html).

Whitemore, T. C. *An Introduction to Tropical Rain Forests*. Oxford, UK: Oxford University Press, 1998.

Whitemore, T. C. *Tropical Deforestation and Species Extinction*. London: Chapman Hall, 1992.

INDEX

A

adaptation to environment, 23, 32–35
Africa, 5, 17, 21, 37, 40
Amazon River basin, 17, 45
Australia, 10, 21

B

birds, 7, 15, 25, 27, 29–30, 32, 35–36
Brazil, 9, 10, 45, 51

D

deforestation, 47–55
desert, 7, 17, 20, 47
desertification, 47
drought, 12, 22

E

elephants, 7, 19, 30
epiphytes, 23
equator, on maps and globes, 5, 6, 9
extinction, 35–37, 52–53
  rate of, 35, 37, 52, 53

G

grasses, 12, 20, 21, 22, 25
greenhouse effect and global warming, 48–50

I

India, 10, 21
Indo-Malaysia, 17
Indonesia, 5, 10
insects, 7, 25, 31–32, 34

J

jaguars, 7, 27, 31, 36

K

Kenya, 7, 10, 13, 41, 44

L

latitude, 5, 9, 11
lions, 30–31, 42

M

Masai, 41–42, 44
Masai Mara National Reserve, 13
medicinal plants, 24

N

Northern Hemisphere, 9, 10, 11
North Pole, 5, 17, 27

P

people living near the equator, 39–45
primates, 7, 27, 36

About the Author

Stephanie Lazor graduated with degrees in English and writing. She currently works in communications for a public relations firm in New York City.

Photo Credits

Cover © Len Rue, Jr./Photo Researchers, Inc.; pp. 1, 3, 16–17, 46–47 © Luiz C. Marigo/Peter Arnold; pp. 4–5 © Gunter Zeisler/Peter Arnold, Inc.; p. 6 © Geoatlas 2003; pp. 8–9 © Charles V. Angelo/Photo Researchers, Inc.; p. 12 © Aldo Brando/Peter Arnold, Inc.; p. 14 © Peter Arnold/Peter Arnold, Inc.; pp. 18, 49, 54 © Jacques Janqoux/Peter Arnold, Inc.; p. 20 © Raghu S. Chundawat/Peter Arnold, Inc.; p. 21 © Kevin Schafer/Corbis; p. 22 © Photo Researchers, Inc.; p. 24 © Walter H. Hodge/Peter Arnold, Inc.; pp. 26–27 © Bios (M & C Denis-Hoot)/Peter Arnold, Inc.; p. 28 © Gerard Lacz/Peter Arnold, Inc.; p. 30 © Dante Fenolo/Photo Researchers, Inc.; p. 31 © George Holton/ Photo Researchers, Inc.; p. 33 © Ed Reschke/Peter Arnold, Inc.; p. 36 © Michael Sewell/ Peter Arnold, Inc.; pp. 38–39 © Ricardo Azoury/Corbis; p. 41 © Victor Englebert/Photo Researchers, Inc.; p. 43 © Jim Zuckerman/ Corbis; p. 51 © Bud Lehnhausen/Photo Researchers, Inc.

Designer: Thomas Forget; Editor: Annie Sommers;
Photo Researcher: Adriana Skura